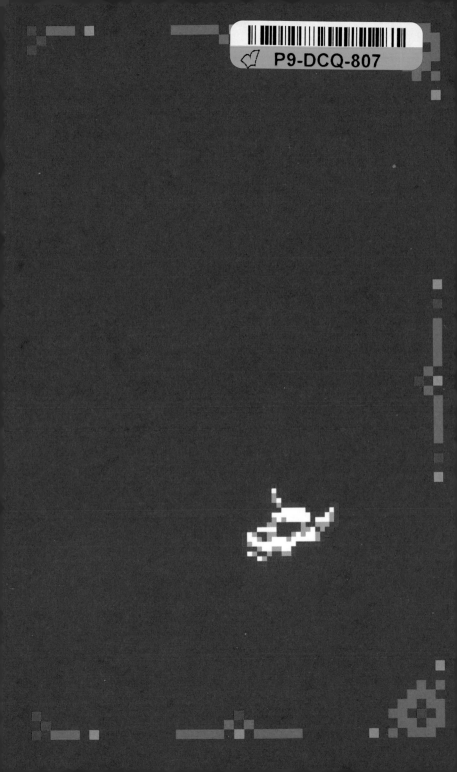

P9-DCQ-807

...AND THEN YOU DIE OF DYSENTERY

Lessons in Adulting from

THE OREGON TRAIL™

...AND THEN YOU DIE OF DYSENTERY

LAUREN REEVES

Illustrated by **JUDE BUFFUM**

Houghton Mifflin Harcourt
Boston   New York
2018

For information about permission to reproduce selections from this book,
write to trade.permissions@hmhco.com or to Permissions, Houghton Mifflin Harcourt
Publishing Company, 3 Park Ave, 19th Floor, New York, New York 10016.

www.hmhco.com

Library of Congress Cataloging-in-Publication Data is available.
ISBN 978-1-328-62439-0

Book design by Christopher Moisan

Printed in the United States of America

DOC 10 9 8 7 6 5 4 3 2 1

INTRODUCTION

You never forget the first time you die. For me, it was at the age of 7, when I was hit with a terrible case of dysentery. I'll spare you the details, but let's just say I was gone within minutes. My tombstone read: "Here lies L, she went to Hell." (Trust me, it *killed* in the second grade.) And from that moment, I was hooked on the Oregon Trail.

I grew up in the majestic state of Alaska, where my favorite thing to do was sit inside and play games on my Grandma's turquoise iMac G3. The Oregon Trail was the perfect escape for me (although it's not like I had many options, considering I lived in darkness and subzero temperatures for nine months out of the year). Forget the educational portion of it — a game where you could break bones, buy ammo to shoot wild animals like a small psychopath, *and* watch your haters die off one by one?! For an indoor kid like me, this was the one-stop shop for living out your wildest fantasies, all from the safety of your computer.

If you were also raised on the Oregon Trail, then congratulations: you, too, are old AF. But we've made it this far, and perhaps it's because when life gets hard, we already know how to ration our food and play this bitch at a grueling pace. At this very moment, you're probably stirring up buried memories from the trail. Like fighting with your siblings over whose turn it was next, or remembering the crush you sat by in the computer lab who was *sooo* impressed when you shot all those buffalo. Remember how rich you felt starting off as a banker with $1,600? Now you don't even have that much in your checking account.

I must've logged ten thousand hours on this thing, making me one of the world's leading Oregon Trail experts. I didn't just play the Oregon Trail, no . . . I *studied* it. And now I want to share some of the important lessons I learned and applied to my everyday life. Like how watching the pioneers migrate from Missouri to Oregon for a better life motivated me to move from Alaska to New York City. Or how shooting wild animals is kind of fucked up, but in some circumstances, it's either that or go vegan, and that would probably kill me. Hell, it even taught me that dying builds character, especially when you do it over and over and in so many different ways. And I bet it taught you something, too.

If this book teaches you just one thing, it's that the Oregon Trail didn't just show you how to die. It also taught you how to *live*. And I hope that inspires you to upgrade your life from a lowly Greenhorn to an Adventurer. Swipe this page left to continue along the trail.

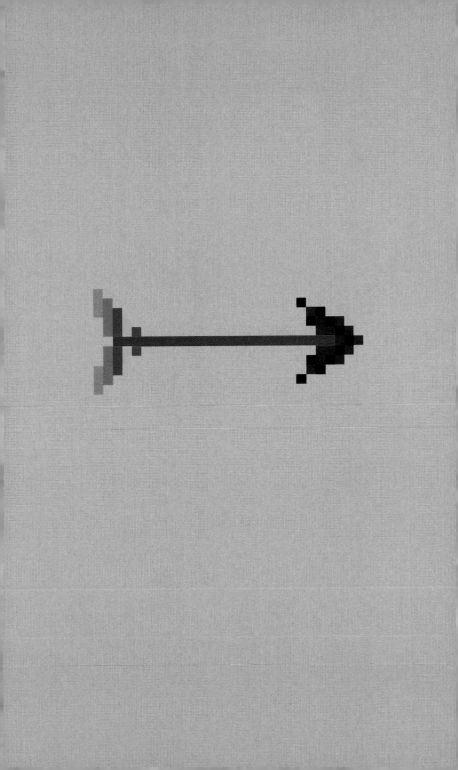

The trail to Oregon is very risky,
and there's a chance you might not make it.
But if you stay in Missouri you could
suffer an even worse fate…

… a serious case of FOMO.

Expect to pay full price

at Matt's General Store…

…unless you're an influencer.

#sponsored #ad

HELLO
MY NAME IS

Assfce

Have fun choosing the names of your party,
but remember you have only a limited
number of spaces.

Feel free to get creative.

Picking which month to depart is
one of the most important decisions
you'll make, and everyone
has an opinion about it.

Ignore the haters.

You can be anything you want—
as long as it's a banker, farmer, or teacher.

Remember, bankers have no useful skills,
only money. Those one percenters will
just try to *buy* their way to Oregon.

Deal with your haters by naming
your wagon party after them.

Sorry you got diphtheria and died, Janice!

Keep a log of everything that happens.

Having a broken leg will get a lot of likes.

This trip is going to take months,
and you'll be sharing tight quarters
with other people in your wagon.

Manspreaders, be warned.

Most days, you'll have to walk 30 miles.

And that's an important reminder
to always get your steps in.

Some places don't need a filter.

Hashtag Chimney Rock.

#ChimneyRock #Nofilter

#WeMadeIt

#WellSomeOfUsDid

Be patient with your family.
You're stuck with them.

But if they do really start to get
on your nerves, have them ford the river.
Somebody's bound to drown!

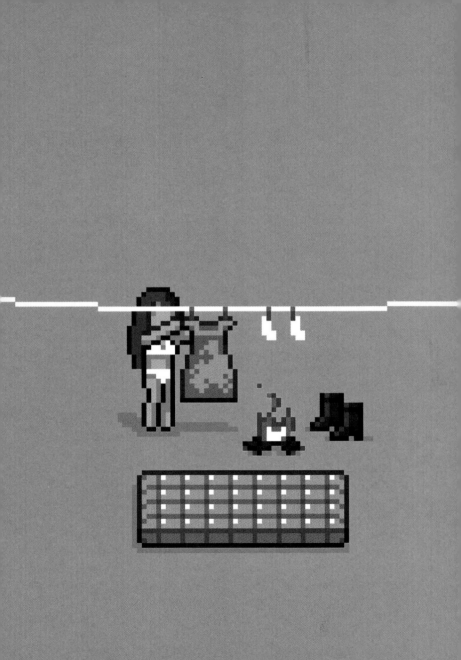

Learn to appreciate life as a minimalist.

It's a lifestyle you've been forced to adopt since you're broke AF.

FORD
THE
RIVER

ME

$5
FERRY
FEE

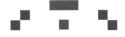

You'll be forced to make decisions that could impact the safety of your family.

Don't get distracted by convenience.

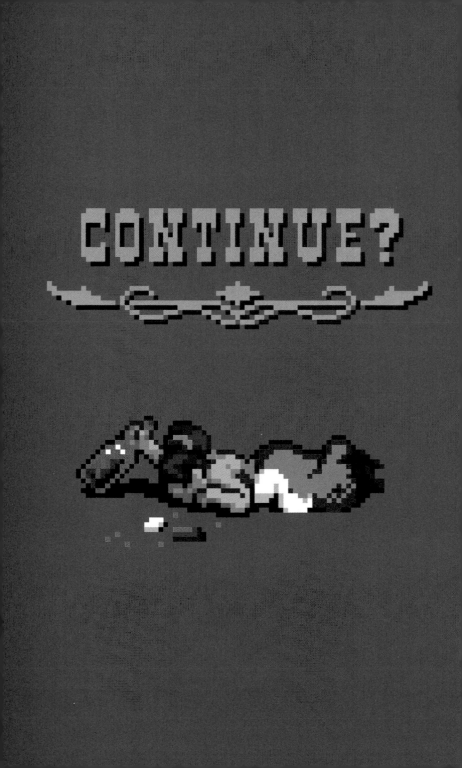

Suffering from exhaustion is a real thing.

It's not just PR code for why
a celebrity went to rehab.

Invite your sweetie to cuddle with you
while looking up at the stars.

The night sky was the original Netflix and chill.
Step 1: Loosen up Orion's belt...

ETA
OCTOBER

Picking up stragglers along the way
can be helpful, especially if they offer
money for the inconvenience.

But this isn't Uber Pool, buddy!
So get your own damn wagon! Zero stars!

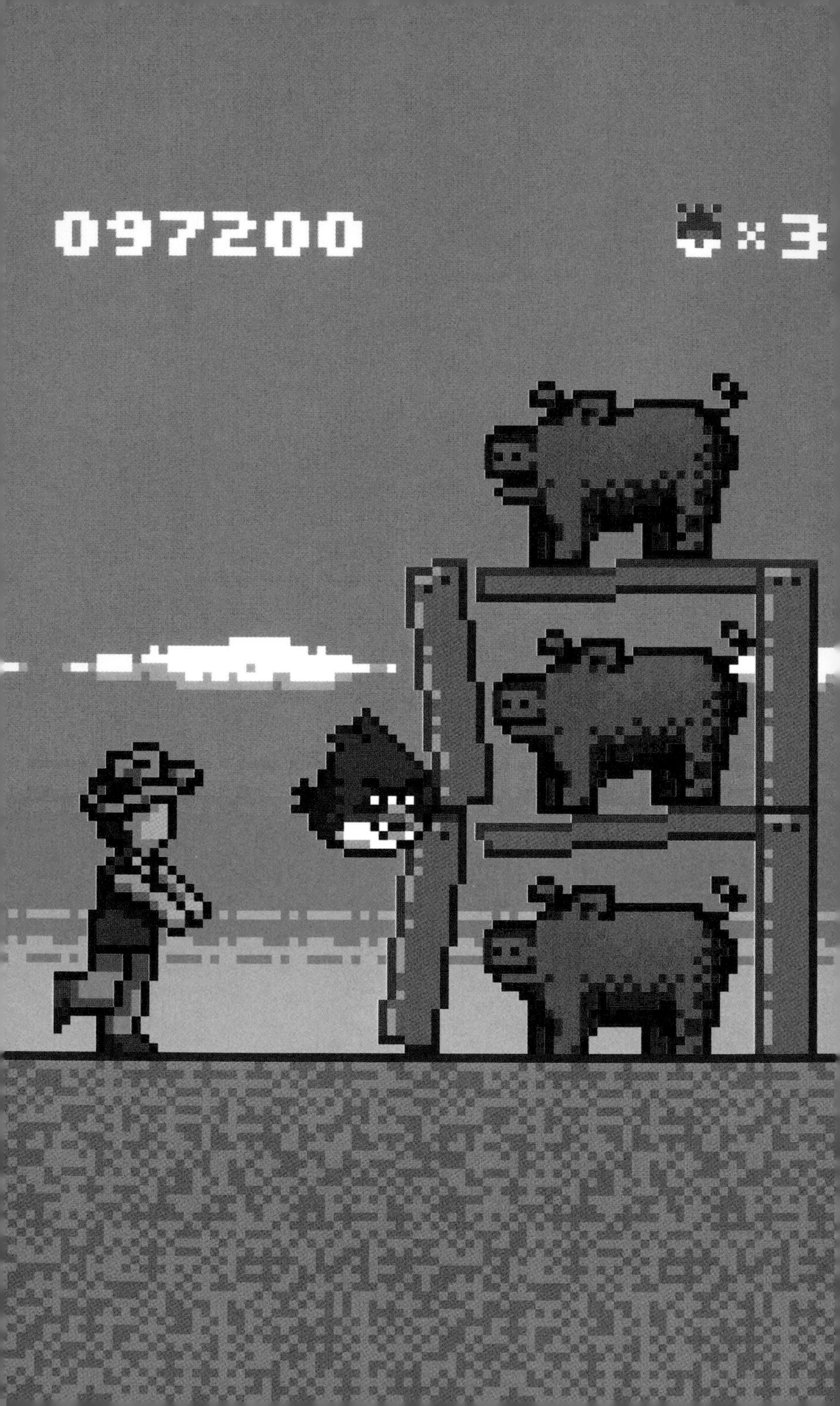
097200
×3

It's important to play games along the trail
to keep yourself entertained.

— Sent from my iPhone

Bad news is best delivered swiftly,
like a rattlesnake bite.

Anyway, Timmy's dead.

The price of supplies and food skyrockets
the closer you get to Oregon.

Two words: Costco. Membership.

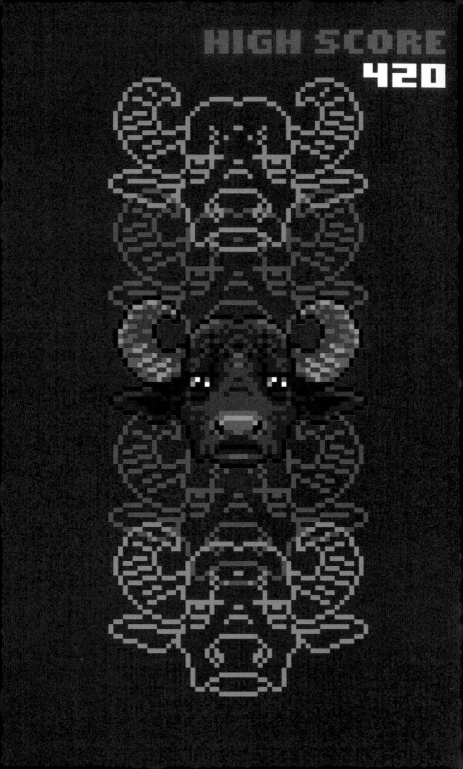

Oxen can die from inadequate grass...

...which is why we need to #LegalizeIt.

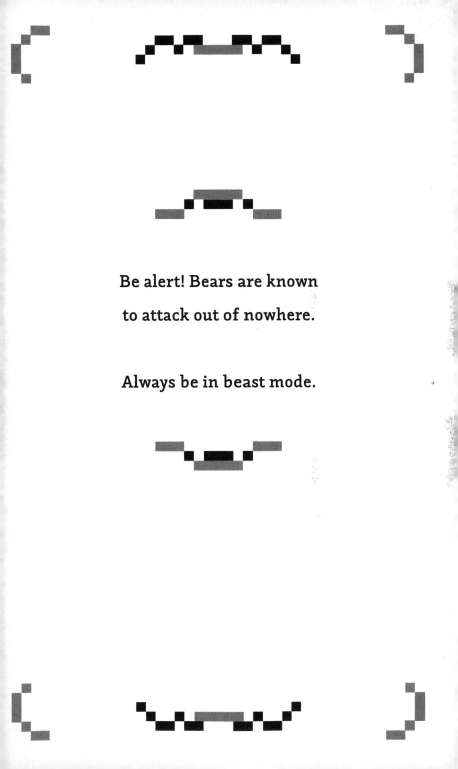

Be alert! Bears are known
to attack out of nowhere.

Always be in beast mode.

CHOLERA

DIPHTHERIA

DYSENTERY

It's possible to get typhoid, cholera, dysentery, measles, *and* diphtheria on one trip.

Gotta catch 'em all!

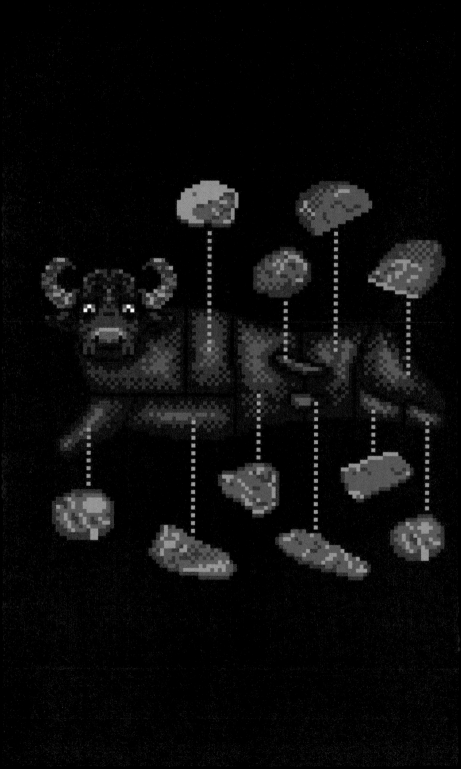

Always eat what you kill,

and only kill what you need.

Unless you're vegan.

In which case:

good luck out there, honey!

Life is full of options: continue on trail, check supplies, look at a map, change your pace, change food rations, stop to rest, attempt to trade, talk to people...

... and of course, curse the heavens.

Dying from a broken arm is possible.

And that's why you should
check WebMD obsessively at the
first sign of soreness.

Don't forget the oxen are the real ones

keeping you on pace.

So sit back and relax while the self-driving

vehicle does all the work.

If you're desperate, you can trade
one set of clothing for one oxen.

It's not exactly a fair deal, but it's
the original Buffalo Exchange.

Buy spare wagon wheels to take on the trip;
you never know when you'll break down.

Love, Mom.

Always take the depth and width of a river

into consideration before crossing it.

YOLO!

It's not unusual to have kids in
your wagon party. And if they act up,
it's okay to punish them.

"Don't make me cut your rations!"

Be prepared for dramatic changes
in the weather.

Blizzards can happen in any climate,
especially when you're surrounded
by liberal snowflakes.

Learn to eat off the land — there's no processed food along the Oregon Trail.

The only Golden Arches here come from the sun setting over the mountains.

Freak accidents can happen
at any time, without warning.

Savage!!

You will break your arms and legs
multiple times on the trip.

And if you can't afford to fix them,
crowdsource the money.

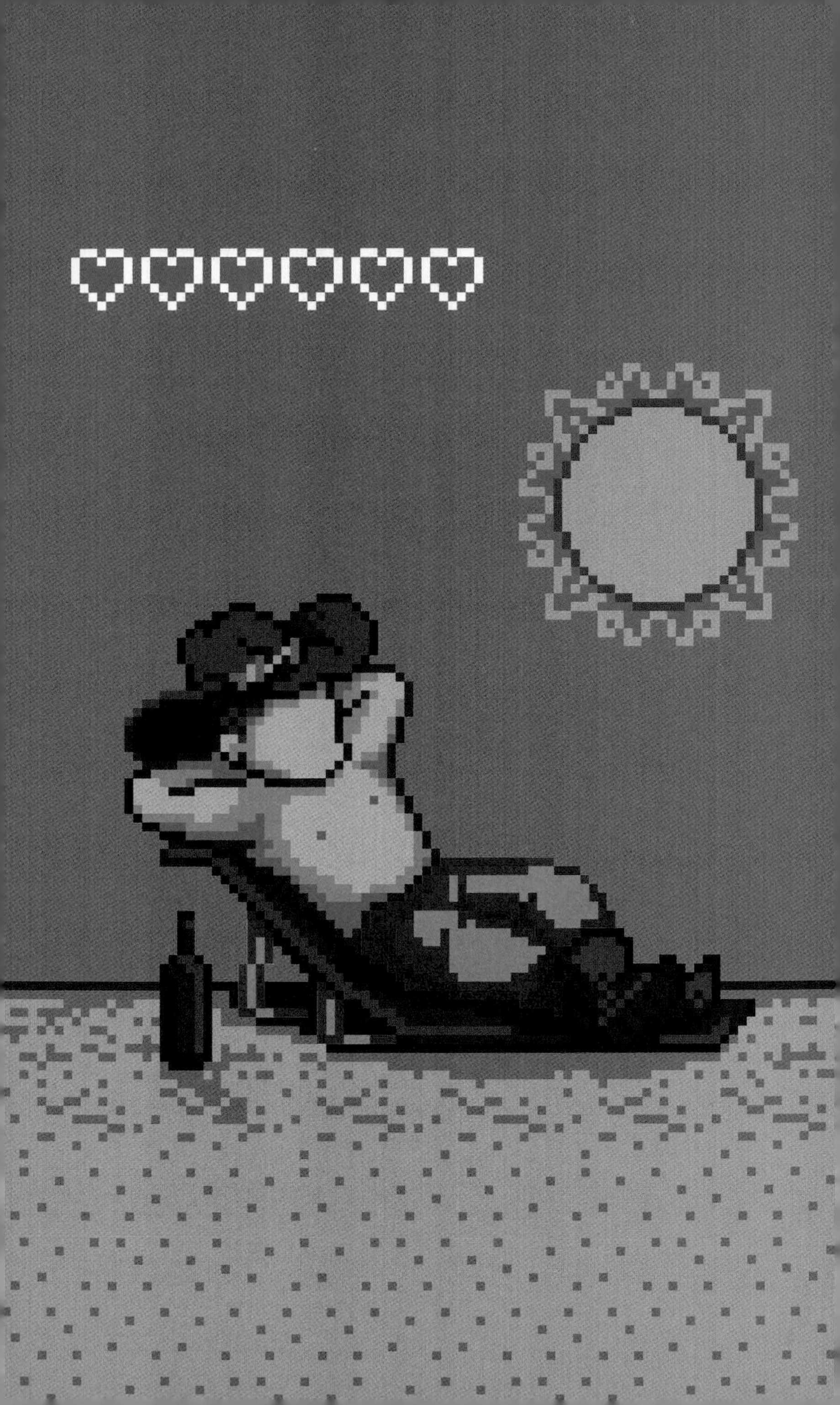

Keep your health up by taking rest days.

Make a staycation out of it

and go glamping.

If you hunt too frequently in one area,
game will become scarce.

The first signs of gentrification.

Read through the trail journal
to reflect on how far you've come.

But don't scroll too far
or you might get trolled.

You left Chimney Rock.
Jareb has a broken leg.
You found some wild berries.
Jareb has cholera.
You found a wagon wheel.
There's no grass for the oxen.
Jareb ugly AF.

Respect the Native Americans
you encounter along the trail...

...by not recognizing Columbus Day
as a national holiday.

Reading that all the members of your

wagon have died teaches you

how to mourn the death of loved ones...

...by simply pressing the space bar to continue.

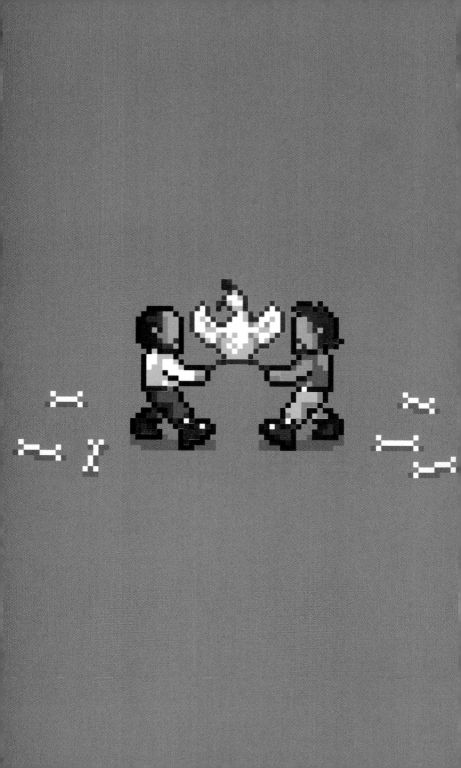

Always keep an eye on your rations.

Because you know what happens

when you get hangry.

If you're not careful, thieves
will ransack your wagon and steal ammo,
oxen, and food while you sleep.

So hide your kids; hide your wife.

Realize that sometimes it's worth it to pay the price of admission — even if you're forced to overpay.

Martin Shkreli has nothing on this guy.

You find out that Perci has a broken leg
and typhoid fever.

Everyone has that one friend who is so extra.

If you're trying to make it to Oregon
before winter, play at a grueling pace.

It's like going on a caffeine binge
the night before a deadline.

When times get hard, push through.
You might have just enough resources
to make it to Oregon.

Don't give up.  Clap. Back.

Sometimes, you're the only survivor
to make it to your destination.

That's some serious adulting.
It's a step above paying rent on time.

Jude Buffum IS WITH
A$$fcc and Janice

MADE IT TO OREGON
October 12, 1852

Celebrate a healthy change of scenery.

A humblebrag on Facebook works well.

Congrats! You made it to Oregon!

It's still fashionable to dress like a pioneer:

you just have to put a bird on it.

And on the rare occasion the entire party
makes it all the way to Oregon, it's okay
to break out in song and dance.

Started from Missouri, now we here.
Started from Missouri, now the
whole team f*ckin' here.

LAUREN REEVES is a comedy writer, actress, and TV host. She was born and raised on a goldmine in Fairbanks, Alaska, leaving at the age of twenty for New York City. Lauren has appeared regularly on the *Late Show with David Letterman* and *Late Night with Jimmy Fallon*, and has worked for shows including Comedy Central's *@Midnight*, TBS's *The Detour*, the Clio Awards, and the *Village Voice* Pride Awards. She currently lives in Los Angeles with her golden retriever, Perci. He wrote this book, not her.

JUDE BUFFUM is an artist from Philadelphia. His illustration and design has received awards from *Graphis, Communication Arts*, AIGA, *3x3, PRINT*, the Society of Illustrators, and *American Illustration*, and has been exhibited internationally.